Little
Pebble™

Little Critters

Honeybees

by Lisa J. Amstutz

CAPSTONE PRESS
a capstone imprint

Little Pebble is published by Capstone Press,
1710 Roe Crest Drive, North Mankato, Minnesota 56003
www.mycapstone.com

Library of Congress Cataloging-in-Publication Data
Names: Amstutz, Lisa J., author.
Title: Honeybees / by Lisa Amstutz.
Other titles: Little pebble. Little critters.
Description: North Mankato, Minnesota : Capstone Press, a Capstone imprint,
   [2018] | Series: Little pebble. Little critters | Audience: Ages 4–8. |
   Audience: K to grade 3. | Includes bibliographical references and index.
Identifiers: LCCN 2016042768| ISBN 9781515778233 (library binding) | ISBN
   9781515778363 (pbk.) | ISBN 9781515778400 (eBook PDF)
Subjects: LCSH: Honeybee—Juvenile literature.
Classification: LCC SF523.5 .A57 2018 | DDC 595.79/9—dc23
LC record available at https://lccn.loc.gov/2016042768

Editorial Credits
Gena Chester, editor; Sarah Bennett, designer;
Wanda Winch, media researcher; Tori Abraham, production specialist

Photo Credits
Dreamstime: Inventori, 11; Shutterstock: Maciej Olszewski, cover, Barsan ATTILA, 15, Billion Photos, 3, 24, Daniel Prudek, 7, Darios, 17, Fotopb.peter, 22, Mirko Graul, 19, 21, muratart, 1, NattyPTG, meadow background, Serg64, 5, szefei, 13, Who What When Where Why Wector, 9

Table of Contents

Busy Bees

Buzz!

There goes a honeybee!

It is looking for food.

Honeybees are insects.

They have six legs.

They have three main
body parts.

head

thorax

abdomen

7

Bees live in a hive.

They have many jobs to do.

The hive is always busy.

Ouch!

Most bees can sting.

They keep the hive safe.

Sweet as Honey

Bees fly to flowers.

Slurp!

They sip nectar.

It is sweet.

The bees fly home.

They put nectar in the hive.

It turns into honey.

15

Bees eat honey in winter.

People like to eat it too.

Yum!

Growing Up

A queen bee lays eggs.

Larvae hatch out.

They look like worms.

larvae

A cocoon covers each larva.

Soon a new bee comes out.

It goes right to work.

new bee

Glossary

cocoon—a covering made of silky thread; some insects make a cocoon to protect themselves while they change from larvae to pupae

hive—a place where a colony of bees lives; thousands of bees live in one hive

honey—a sweet, sticky substance that honeybees make from nectar

insect—a small animal with a hard outer shell, six legs, three body sections, and two antennae; most insects have wings

larva—an insect at the stage of development between an egg and an adult

nectar—a sweet liquid found in many flowers

Read More

Herrington, Lisa M. *It's a Good Thing There are Bees.* Rookie Read-About Science. New York: Children's Press, 2015.

Marsico, Katie. *Honey Bee.* Creepy Crawly Critters. Ann Arbor, Mich.: Cherry Lake Publishing, 2015.

Martin, Isabel. *Insects: A Question and Answer Book.* Animal Kingdom Questions and Answers. North Mankato, Minn.: Capstone Press, 2015.

Internet Sites

FactHound offers a safe, fun way to find Internet sites related to this book. All of the sites on FactHound have been researched by our staff.

Here's all you do:
Visit *www.facthound.com*
Type in this code: 9781515778233

Super-cool stuff!

Check out projects, games and lots more at
www.capstonekids.com

Critical Thinking Questions

1. What do honeybees eat?
2. How do honeybees make honey?
3. How do bees protect themselves?

Index